1.Edition 2023
ISBN 978-82-693178-0-0 (Paperback)
ISBN 978-82-693178-1-7 (Hardcover)
ISBN 978-82-693178-2-4 (Ebook)
Published by 4DIGITS AS

"Give people what they need:
food, medicine, clean air, pure water, trees
and grass, pleasant homes to live in, some
hours of work, more hours of leisure. Don't
ask who deserves it. Every human being
deserves it."

Howard Zinn, Marx in Soho

A car – and the art of maintaining a body

- 5 life hacks that guarantee you a better and longer life

By

Alf Erik Malm

Table of Content

Introduction

When it comes to body goals or mental freedom, we want it NOW. If you ask me, I would say it's an understandable demand or heart desire. Now one really wants to be overweight for a long or battle with mental health illness for months. It's not a good place to be, and it's okay if you want your result as fast as possible. I'm here to show you how to get that.

Countless and random online hacks will tell you to follow this guide, take this drink, or even go on a 3-5 day fruit fast to lose some pounds, but they will not look deeper into who you are and help you schedule a process that works best for you.

While I understand the desire and requirement for a fast result, I also understand the innate desire to enjoy this result longer and the requirement for such a result to come naturally without harming a single hair on your head. I have good news in this regard, it's possible, and you can do it.

You can get in shape, burn enough calories, lose some fat, and embrace mental freedom. The hidden truth is that body size and mental health are two of the most complicated and relatively intertwined conditions, so connected that there is hardly a way to experience one without another.

Today, taking in a lot of food is easy without caring so much. We don't get to check the calories every time, but the pizza tastes great, and we even have a burger in our favorite lunch pack. It's tasty, and we can't even imagine a day without one of those processed and fat-dense snacks that do not fill the tummy and leave us craving more food.

I know it's hard to live free of that food, but the magic you are not seeing is that it is also damn affordable. You won't spend so much on excellent fruit and a plate of pasta, but can you consider how much the McDonald's Burger cost? With the price you just saw, I assume we are now on the same page: healthy meals are affordable and health-friendly.

In this book, I'll tell the story you love to hear, share experiences, and show why making friendly choices for yourself is the best act of freedom and self-love anyone can enjoy. By the end of this book, I'm more than confident that you will start setting body goals and preferred weight and making plans to achieve them.

A Car

For some moments, imagine that you are 17 years old and have your whole adult life ahead of you. You are healthy, fast, and have a great appetite and confidence. Wake up every day to the regular task and the youthful affirmation of a good and beautiful life full of opportunities, and like one of those opportunities, you get an offer you can't refuse. An offer you only get once in a lifetime.

You can choose a brand-new car and get it completely free. No one is taking the task of picking the car, so the offer allows you to pick any car, even the car you want most of all. You have to say the name. However, the offer comes with a caveat. You must agree to ride this car for the rest of your life. So it's not just an ordinary car; it's a car for a lifetime.

Now that you have this one-in-a-lifetime offer of picking out any car in the world that money can buy, what will you go for?

Yes, it is tricky, but you definitely don't want to miss out on getting a free ride when you can choose the most expensive or fanciest ride and enjoy it for the rest of your life.

The cheeky sports car you have a picture of in the boys' room? Or would you be able to think ahead and consider that it will be a little impractical when you have a family and are going on a cabin trip? What about a motor home? What about durability? It is no doubt that some cars maintain a higher quality than others. Now that the stress of considering the price and checking if it is something you can afford, considering your financial status, is off the table before you make the decision, you need to set up some points that will be decisive for your choice.

If I'm the one choosing this ride, I'll be considering the following:
- Quality
- Good space and storage facilities
- Design
- Big engine
- Maintenance costs
- Consumption

Since I'm more grown now, I'm sure if I'm presented with such a chance right, I would probably choose an SUV from one of Europe's leading manufacturers if you ask me today. It would cover my family and my needs. Full of extras and with the biggest engine that could be offered. But will I make a similar decision as a 17-year-old? I'm not sure. More than an SUV, I am more convinced that I'll be considering a Porche 911 or the Lamborghini Diablo that I had a poster of in my room when I was 17. Yes, let's say I had chosen a red Diablo.

How do you think that car would look today, 33 years later?

If you're going to have a car like that for the rest of your life. How would you care for it? For my 17-year-old self, I'm sure I've some of the best plans in place for my favorite car. For instance, I would probably create a maintenance plan that looks like this:

1. Service once per year
2. Washed and boned regularly
3. Tectyl treatment every 5 years
4. Never let it run out of fuel
5. Replace the battery if there are signs of reduced power
6. Changed cables that showed signs of wear/aging
7. Fixed bugs immediately
8. Regularly check wearing parts
9. Change the oil regularly
10. Fixed paint damage and stone chips immediately.

My first car was a Volkswagen Golf CL 1982 model. I bought it as a used car in 1992. It was blue, had 5 seats and was perfect for me. After a couple of years, I sold the car for half of what I bought it for, and its condition was not optimal. When I checked public records, I saw that the car was condemned the day before Christmas Eve in 1997.

What does your first car look like?
And what does this have to do with health?

The human body requires servicing and maintenance just like a car does. However, at a younger age, we are more likely to take reckless steps without considering how long our bodies can last. Just like I realized my 17 years old self would have chosen a Porche 911 or Lamborghini, I learned many people take less care of their bodies at a younger age. No one cares about what is practical or the consequence of binge eating, continued alcohol, and constant smoking. It's fun, and everyone is doing it is the only reason we need to get started.

However, the human body responds to situations as a car does. When the situation changes and you're married, the fancy Porche becomes highly impractical and is no longer the best ride to enjoy a long trip with families and friends. You will need a new car, preferably an SUV, to enjoy the journey with your family in one place.

The case is similar for the body. You want to look good, you want to perform well, you want to move well, and you also don't want to break down. You don't want to undergo constant repairs. And end up with a knee replacement, a hip replacement, or some of your organs taken out. Then you need to start paying adequate attention to the type of body you choose, the plans you put in place to maintain such a body, and the things that may hinder you from enjoying that body.

Will you choose a fancy body or a durable one? Will you consume all the alcohol, take the shot, smoke every time and ditch all maintenance plans or will you check your daily routine, pick the best body, and stick to maintenance plans?

Who am I?

This year I am turning 50, and here is my debut as a writer. My goal with this book is that you pick up a thing or two making your life better and longer. In my day job, I work to increase the quality of life for people with a disease or who have been in an accident. But this book offers improved quality of life to all.

It is no coincidence that I work in this field. This is what gives my engine full throttle. And of course, sports then, primarily when competing myself, but also by watching others. In the last decade, I have attended many competitions as an athlete. I've participated in several organized activities like running, skiing, and cycling, mostly triathlons. I've done everything from small local events to Ironman and Norseman, which is probably the most challenging triathlon in the world.

I have 5 children and 2 grandchildren. I am blessed with a fabulous wife and good friends. I eat healthily and regularly. These elements are the basics in my life and a recipe for high quality and long life.

Days in the army

I have always loved doing sports, from football, Ice hockey to boxing, running, and other races. When I went to high school, I chose the line of sports, training 2 times a day and about 15-20 hours a week.

At age 17, the army summoned all Norwegians to a test day. They test your knowledge level, physical level, and your motivation to be in the military. I had a good day and did well in the knowledge and physical tests. My weight was 74 kilos distributed over 183 centimeters. It did not take many weeks before I got a letter that I was drafted into the Navy for the first service of 12 months. When I finished high school, my motivation for training was low. I did not have goals and was tired of many years of training. I decided to take a break from training. I got a girlfriend, and we enjoyed the evenings watching films. I had always needed a lot of food, so I continued eating. Then my girlfriend got pregnant, and my focus shifted.

Two years after the initial test, I started my service in the Navy. At the recruit school, the first week I was tested again. My shape was far from exceptional, and my weight was 94 kilos. It is not easy to run fast or walk with a backpack for 2 days with 20 kilos extra on the body. My weight was down to 82 kilos after 6 weeks of high activity and not much food. The army gave me a helping hand in getting back on track. Today, 30 years later, my weight is 78 kilos.

"Health is not valued until sickness comes."
Thomas Fuller

What it means to be Overweight ?

Being overweight is simply a stage where the body weighs more than what is proportionate to age or height. A lot of things can affect a person's weight and weight fluctuation. The body and the head are connected. What you eat and drink, how much you sleep, how much you move, whether you smoke, and other small choices you make every day have something to say for your brain, your heart, your skin and hair, and for how you experience life's adversity or prosperity as the case may be.

So, let's look at the status of our bodies.

Overweight

Overweight and obesity are defined as abnormal or excessive fat accumulation that may impair health. Body mass index (BMI) is a simple weight-for-height index commonly used to classify overweight and obesity in adults. It is defined as a person's weight in kilograms divided by the square of his height in meters (kg/m2).

How to calculate your Body Mass Index (BMI)

Height: 175cm, Weight: 80 kg. 80/(1,75x1,75=3,06) 3,06= BMI 26,1

For adults, the WHO defines overweight and obesity as follows:

- overweight is a BMI greater than or equal to 25; and
- obesity is a BMI greater than or equal to 30.

Hence, when calculated, anyone with a BMI of 25 or greater is considered overweight, while those with 30 or greater BMI are obese.

The prevalence of this problem is notably a significant issue across nations. For instance, a report shows that Iceland had the highest number of obese or overweight by 58.5% in 2019. While many individuals can keep their bodies in check and embrace a healthy lifestyle, some cannot meet body demands. People consume more and more foods that add excessively to their body weight every day, from junk food to high fatty acid foods.

Notable, the United States Department Of Health And Human Services reported in June 2021 that among adults aged 20 and over, the age-adjusted prevalence of obesity was 41.9%, and severe obesity was 9.2%.

Furthermore, the Health Survey for England 2019, published in 2020, reported that 27% of men and 29% of women were obese. Around two-thirds of adults were overweight or obese. This was more prevalent among men (68%) than women (60%).

Also, Statista reported that the total number of overweight adults (those aged 18 years and above) worldwide amounted to 2 billion as of 2019. And most of us believe that number increased a lot during the pandemic.

Consequences of being overweight

Being overweight or obese exposes people to a certain level of risk, some of which can notably lead to death or mental health issues. Let's discuss them below

Type 2 diabetes

The condition most strongly influenced by body weight is type 2 diabetes. In the Nurses' Health Study, which followed 114,000 middle-aged women for 14 years, the risk of developing diabetes was 93 times higher among women who had a body mass index (BMI) of 35 or higher at the start of the study, compared with women with BMIs lower than 22.

Cardiovascular Disease

Body weight is directly associated with various cardiovascular risk factors. As BMI increases, so do blood pressure, low-density lipoprotein (LDL, or "bad")

cholesterol, triglycerides, blood sugar, and inflammation. These changes translate into increased risk for coronary heart disease, stroke, and cardiovascular death:

Depression

A meta-analysis of 15 long-term studies that followed 58,000 participants for up to 28 years found that people who were obese at the start had a 55 percent higher risk of developing depression by the end of the follow-up period. People who had depression at the beginning of the study had a 58 percent higher risk of becoming obese.

Cancer

An expert panel assembled by the World Cancer Research Fund and the American Institute for Cancer Research concluded that there was convincing evidence of an association between obesity and cancers of the esophagus, pancreas, colon and rectum, breast, endometrium, and kidney, and a possible association between obesity and gallbladder cancer.

Reproduction

Obesity can influence various aspects of reproduction, from sexual activity to conception. Among women, the association between obesity and infertility, primarily ovulatory infertility, is represented by a classic U-shaped curve. In the Nurses' Health Study, infertility was lowest in women with BMIs between 20 and 24 and increased with lower and higher BMIs. (20) This study suggests that 25 percent of ovulatory infertility in the United States may be attributable to obesity.

Lung Function/Respiratory Disease
Asthma and obstructive sleep are two common respiratory diseases linked to obesity.

Musculoskeletal Disorders
Excess weight places mechanical and metabolic strains on bones, muscles, and joints. In the United States, an estimated 46 million adults (about one in five) report doctor-diagnosed arthritis. Osteoarthritis of the knee and hip is positively associated with obesity, and obese patients account for one-third of all joint replacement operations. Obesity also increases the risk of back pain, lower limb pain, and disability due to musculoskeletal conditions.

My Body; My Car

You've not forgotten about my car. The not impractical but yet highly desired Lamborghini Diablo I told I'd choose as a 17 years teenager. Let's think of how I can manage it to make the best of it. Even if I won't be able to take my family on a trip in this car, it is fancy enough for several occasions, and I love to leave people speechless.

Do you think I will overuse my car, put it on a roof rack, and use it to transport water cans? If you were the owner of that fancy Lamborghini, would you put more weight than recommended in your car?

I certainly won't do that. Even though I didn't start with the most suitable car for later years, I will not want to use it anyhow, constantly put loads on it, and overuse it without any yearly service or maintenance plan.

Put your body in this position and see how it plays out. We won't necessarily start great, but we can take the required steps to get on the right track.

Life is a series of events, moments, mistakes, and grieves captured in what is called "process." The most beautiful thing I've realized is the fact no matter how mistakenly constructed, no matter the errors and the many tries, the process is not an optimal definition of who we are or the life we can live. Many of us won't get it right at the start, and many will wander off the right track, but we can make mistakes and implement necessary corrections is one of the most magical powers we hold as humans.

Yes, there are years of smoking and constant consumption of alcohol. Perhaps, you are made to deal with so much stress that you cannot help but find fortitude and peace in alcohol; however, this should not determine how you treat your body.

As we grow older, we may understand that grieving is unnecessary and that some pain is meant to come. Moments that teach us the most important lessons are not usually palatable. We must go through stress and sometimes pain to make a good life for ourselves. However, in the middle of all the daily tolling and tons of tasks, we may shift to things that are not inherently beneficial only for the moment.

Irrespective of where your body is, you can consciously keep it safe and regain all the bliss you've lost. Remember when I said I weighed 94 kg? I was shocked, but I didn't stay there for too long, and with constant activities, I lost 12 kg in 6 weeks and eventually achieved a healthy body again.

"I believe that the greatest gift you can give your family and the world is a healthy you."

Joyce Meyer

What can Physical Activity do for You?

WHO defines physical activity as any bodily movement produced by skeletal muscles that require energy expenditure. Physical activity refers to all movement, including during leisure time, for transport to and from places or as part of a person's work. Both moderate- and vigorous-intensity physical activity improve health. Popular ways to be active include walking, cycling, wheeling, sports, active recreation, and play, and they can be done at any level of skill and for enjoyment by everybody.

Regular physical activity is proven to help prevent and manage non-communicable diseases such as heart disease, stroke, diabetes, and several cancers. It also helps prevent hypertension, maintains healthy body weight, and improves mental health, quality of life, and well-being.

Prevalence of adults aged 18+ years not meeting WHO physical activity guidelines.

	Females 18-44 years	Females 45-69 years	Males 18-44 years	Males 45-69 years
African region	19 %	25 %	10 %	18 %
American region	40 %	49 %	28 %	37 %
Eastern Mediterranean Region	43 %	49 %	22 %	30 %
South-East Asia region	35 %	41 %	18 %	26 %
Western Pacific Region	16 %	19 %	15 %	21 %
European Region	28 %	32 %	20 %	30 %

The chart shows the percentage of adults (over 18 years) who are not sticking to the WHO direction regarding the level of physical exercise required per week for a healthy body. As reported by the chart, the African region graph notably shows a lower percentage of people participating in physical activities as directed by WHO. Similarly, the West Pacific Region graph also shows low participation.

The consequence of physical inactivity is not just that it increases people's weight and may lead to obesity. Physical inactivity is estimated to costs the global health systems about US$ 27 billion a year, and by 2030, physical inactivity is projected to cost US$ 300 billion.

Contrary to many perceptions, physical activity does not require much time or money. In the real sense, it is affordable to stay healthy. With just 150 minutes of exercise per week, we can meet the physical activity yardstick suggested by WHO to improve health and keep our bodies safe.

Norseman Triathlon

I'm a fan of sports, and after realizing that it takes sitting sit to gain more than 10kg, I learned to stay active every day. I'm a big fan of a healthy body because if I picked this Lamborghini because it's fancy, I'd realize taking care of it is more important than regretting why I didn't choose an SUV.

Like many people out there, I once forgot about what it feels like to stay healthy, eat healthily, and move around, and for that, I gained over 13 kg of weight in just a few years. However, I do not give up on my body. The one-time mistake will not get the best of me because I know just how much I want to stay agile, even at 70. I have several sports experiences, but the Norseman Triathlon is one of the things you naturally know you cannot forget.

Norseman Xtreme Triathlon is rated as the most challenging triathlon in the world. Their slogan, "This is not for you," sends many people away before trying. However, contrary to what we naturally expect, more people are interested in trying it out. Perhaps, they are all curious or big on sports like I am. Hence, even though the race is hard, getting a start number is harder. Every year 5000 people attend a lottery to get one of the 250 start slots.

By 2021 had tried for six years to get a spot but did not get one. Then the pandemic gave me an opening since some of the athletes could not travel abroad. 6 weeks before the race, I got an email with an invitation to join in and grabbed it without hesitating. Norseman is something special and every triathlete's dream.

The race starts with a 3.8-kilometer swim in a fjord in Norway at 05.00 AM. We were transported by a ferry in the dark, and the sea got heavier and heavier the more we moved from the starting point. Usually, I would use 1 hour and 15 minutes swimming this distance, but this morning, I spent over 2 hours in cold water with challenging waves and currents. On the way to my bike, I felt like I had swallowed a fjord of salt water and was tired and dizzy.

On the bike leg, you start with a 1000-meter climb up a mountain plateau. Entering the plateau, I met a headwind of 20 m/s and some rain. My schedule was already history, and now it was all about finishing. After almost 9 hours on the bike, I had done 180 kilometers and climbed 2800 meters on the bike. I was exhausted and had nothing to eat since the swim. I was cold and wet, but the motivation was still there.

The finish line is on top of a mountain called Gaustadtoppen. It is 1800 meters above sea level, so the climbing was not over. I picked up another athlete sitting freezing in the transition zone, and we decided to finish this together. The rain was constant, but we kept the mood up by sharing our misery. Sometimes one plus one is more than two, and this was one of those moments. At midnight in the dark, we passed the finish line together. The two last ones to finish the race that year, 19 hours after the start. Although all my ambitions for a good result were crushed, I was still proud. Proud to have finished, and to have put myself in a position to undertake such a challenge at the age of 47.

What Causes Overweight or Obesity?

Adding weight is the consequence of several actions, just like staying healthy and keeping your weight below 25 BMI is also a result of several things. Many people wonder why they added so much weight in a short time, but the fact remains that no matter how good your body is if you do not stick to a particular and workable routine to keep it in shape, you will gain weight.

The real enemy of our body is sitting still and doing nothing. The time we spend on the internet doing nothing, the foods we overeat because they taste damn good, and the unhealthy habit that will pick up are all the reasons we add more weight. Hence, it is to say that whatever you let in or do affect the body, either directly or indirectly.

Here are things that can make someone overweight or cause obesity

Mental health

Mental health is a state of mental well-being that enables people to cope with the stresses of life, realize their abilities, learn well and work well, and contribute to their community. It is an integral component of health and well-being that underpins our individual and collective skills to make decisions, build relationships and shape our world. Mental health is a fundamental human right. And it is crucial to personal, community, and socio-economic development.

Mental health is more than the absence of mental disorders. It exists on a complex continuum, experienced differently from one person to the next, with varying degrees of difficulty and distress and potentially very different social and clinical outcomes.

Mental health conditions include mental disorders and psychosocial disabilities as well as other mental states associated with significant distress, impairment in functioning, or risk of self-harm. People with mental health conditions are more likely to experience lower levels of mental well-being, but this is not always or necessarily the case.

How common are mental illnesses?

The truth is our world is chaotic, with several things happening everywhere. War, insecurity, and several societal standards put people on edge and cause them to doubt their ability to stay calm and find themselves.

While the number of affected people may appear minimal,
studies and reports have shown that mental health illness affects more than 50% of the global population. Mental health conditions like depression, anxiety, and more affect many people at one point or another. However, while some can overcome this trouble, others deal with the mitigated version by following therapy guides, self-help tips, and taking medication.

It is a fact that mental illnesses are among the most common health conditions in the United States. The statistical report below shows enough reasons we should be concerned about keeping our mental health safe and sound and also gives us reasons to help and understand those dealing with these issues.

- Over 50% of Americans will have a mental illness at some point in their lifetime.
- 1 in 5 Americans is expected to experience a mental illness in a given year.

- 1 in 5 children, either currently or at some point during their life, have experienced a seriously debilitating mental illness.

- 1 in 25 Americans lives with a severe mental illness, such as schizophrenia, bipolar disorder, or major depression.

Mental illness or mental health disorder can come in different forms causing people to experience different symptoms. For some, the symptoms are similar and may require close professional help to understand and identify the exact type of mental health disorder someone has. Some of the most frequent mental illnesses include depression, anxiety disorders, schizophrenia, eating disorders, and addictive behaviors.

Many people have mental health concerns from time to time. However, a mental health concern becomes a mental illness when ongoing signs and symptoms cause frequent stress and affect your ability to function.

Mental health disorder affects every part of a person's life. When affected, victims often feel more miserable and stressed. This may impact daily life, sexual life, and even relationships. Mental health disorders like depression can cause constant sadness and reduce interest in things you used to like. Anxiety instills fears in you, causing the victim to stop several parts of their lives, like outings, social gatherings, or sexual activities with partners.

In most cases, symptoms can be managed with a combination of medications and talk therapy (psychotherapy).

Signs and symptoms of mental illness can vary depending on the disorder, circumstances, and other factors. Mental illness symptoms can affect emotions, thoughts, and behaviors.

Examples of signs and symptoms include:

- Feeling sad or down

- Confused thinking or reduced ability to concentrate

- Excessive fears or worries or extreme feelings of guilt

- Radical mood changes of highs and lows

- Withdrawal from friends and activities

- Significant tiredness, low energy, or problems sleeping

- Detachment from reality (delusions), paranoia, or hallucinations

- Inability to cope with daily problems or stress

- Trouble understanding and relating to situations and people

- Problems with alcohol or drug use

- Significant changes in eating habits

- Sex drive changes

- Excessive anger, hostility, or violence

- Suicidal thinking

Sometimes symptoms of a mental health disorder appear as physical problems, such as stomach pain, back pain, headaches, or other unexplained aches and pains.

"Happiness lies first of all in health."

George William Curtis

What causes mental illness?

The origin of mental health illness in many people cannot be categorically asserted. Also, people experience mental health issues in different parts of the world occasioned by several factors including, but not limited to, the following

- Early adverse life experiences, such as trauma or a history of abuse (for example, child abuse, sexual assault, witnessing violence, etc.)
- Experiences related to other ongoing (chronic) medical conditions, such as cancer or diabetes
- Biological factors or chemical imbalances in the brain
- Use of alcohol or drugs
- Having feelings of loneliness or isolation

Mental illnesses, in general, are thought to be caused by a variety of genetic and environmental factors:

- **Inherited traits.**
  Mental illness is more common in people whose blood relatives also have a mental illness. Specific genes may increase your risk of developing a mental illness, and your life situation may trigger it.

- **Environmental exposures before birth.**
  Exposure to environmental stressors, inflammatory conditions, toxins, alcohol, or drugs in the womb can sometimes be linked to mental illness.

- **Brain chemistry.**
  Neurotransmitters are naturally occurring brain chemicals that carry signals to other parts of your brain and body. When the neural networks involving these chemicals are impaired, the function of nerve receptors and nerve systems change, leading to depression and other emotional disorders.

Risk factors

Certain factors may increase your risk of developing a mental illness, including:

- A history of mental illness in a blood relative, such as a parent or sibling

- Stressful life situations, such as financial problems, a loved one's death, or a divorce

- An ongoing (chronic) medical condition, such as diabetes

- Brain damage as a result of a severe injury (traumatic brain injury), such as a violent blow to the head

- Traumatic experiences, such as military combat or assault

- Use of alcohol or recreational drugs

- A childhood history of abuse or neglect

- Few friends or few healthy relationships

- A previous mental illness

Complications

Mental illness is a leading cause of disability. Untreated mental illness can cause severe emotional, behavioral, and physical health problems. Complications are sometimes linked to mental illnesses and may be caused by factors like:

- Unhappiness and decreased enjoyment of life

- Family conflicts

- Relationship difficulties

- Social isolation

- Problems with tobacco, alcohol, and other drugs

- Missed work or school, or other issues related to work or school

- Legal and financial problems

- Poverty and homelessness

- Self-harm and harm to others, including suicide or homicide

- The weakened immune system, so your body has a hard time resisting infections

- Heart disease and other medical conditions

Visits to the doctor

The presence of mental health illness is often neglected by many causing them to suffer more pain. Several people do not consider mental health illness a problem, while some are ashamed to accept or share that their minds need more attention. Hence, they muscle through the pain or shoulder it alone.

The fact remains that more and more people are getting affected, and by not visiting the doctor, victims increase the chance of developing other symptoms or escalating the existing signs.

Number of doctor visits per capita in selected countries (2019)

Japan	13 times a year
Italy	10 times a year
Germany	10 times a year
Netherlands	9 times a year
Canada	7 times a year
Australia	7 times a year
France	6 times a year
Spain	5 times a year
UK	5 times a year
Norway	4 times a year
USA	4 times a year

Source: World Health Organization

According to the report above, it's apparent that more Americans are not visiting doctors despite harsh exposure to several factors causing mental health illness. Following the US is the United Kingdom.

Despite the apparent need for mental health victims to visit doctors and attend several therapies for quality results, many victims, particularly in the United either choose not to access the healthcare system or do not even have access to quality medical help.

This constantly contributes to the prevalence of mental health disorders in many people and therefore increases the number of affected persons.

"To keep the body in good health is a duty, otherwise we shall not be able to keep the mind strong and clear."

Buddha

Factors contributing to why many are overweight

Unemployment is a social menace facing several countries with significant negative impacts on unemployed people. Employment is one of the leading causes of mental health disorders in many people. Also, it is substantially responsible for why people sit still and do.

An unemployed person has no business waking up early and engaging in physical activities like going and coming from work. Similarly, there are no office tasks to be completed; hence, they have no reason to go through mental tasking or develop themselves.

As a cause of mental health illness, unemployment can lead to financial instability, economic stress, and unhappiness and may send affected people down into a depressive mode. Consequently, this may prevent them from engaging in random fitness activities to keep their bodies in check.

A great opportunity – MY presentation

In 2016 I was invited by a former colleague to present to an unemployed group. They were part of a program helping them get back to work. My initial idea was that with extra time available, they could use some of it to increase their total package, which would also increase their chance of getting work.

Since I knew that many were economically stressed, I changed my initial presentation with that in mind. I started with diet and exercise, showing them how easy this could be a part of their daily routine without costing more.

Sleep was the next topic, and I was getting feedback that this was a significant issue for many of them. Given that they were not tired in the evening and had no reason to get up early in the morning, they often put themselves in a mentally drained space where mental health becomes a main problem.

Several factors like the inability to meet financial demands to enjoy simple social life like outings, social events, or even trips to fancy and nice locations with friends. They don't often consider resting and may be lost in thought and depressed.

Focusing on the need to rest the brain, get enough sleep and enjoy simple activities without spending a lot of money, I showed them how important it is to manage their mental health and sleep properly.

After the presentation, many attendees contacted me, who wanted to thank me and ask more about when I could come back. A survey made after the presentation gave 85% the feedback that the presentation changed their life to a better one and increased their ability to get back to work.

Even as an unemployed person, you need to take good care of your body because by not doing anything, you expose your body to high risk and the chance of adding more weight since there are no physical activities to burn calories or fat. Hence, it is essential that even when you're not actively working in an office or handling a business, you need to stay physically active to keep your body shape and get it ready for work.

This requirement is not a hard or expensive one. In the real sense, you can engage in countless physical activities to burn calories daily in your house or street. An early morning or late evening jogging will do you better than sitting at home all day. Get out there and enjoy a highly refreshed moment with friends or alone.

Take the evening walk and visit simple fitness events to compete for free.

Disability

A higher percentage of disabled people are exposed to being unemployed because of the natural stereotypical view that they cannot be as efficient as their able counterparts. While this is true in some situations, it is not valid. However, jobs that can be handled perfectly by people with a specific disability are not given to them for general public prejudice.

1 in 5 people of working age is disabled, a total of 20 percent of the working-age living without jobs. Furthermore, about 33 percent of the working-age population is dealing with a long-term health condition, while another 8 percent reportedly have a severe disability.

1 in 5 of the working-age population are classed as disabled

Figure 3a: Proportion of the population with a long-term health condition or disability, people aged 16 to 64, UK, 2020 to 2021

33% of the working-age population report having a long-term health condition

20% of the working-age population report having a disability

8% of the working-age population report having a severe disability

Some health conditions have a bigger impact on day-to-day activities than others

Figure 5: Proportion of people by main health condition and health and disability status, people aged 16 to 64, UK, 2020/21

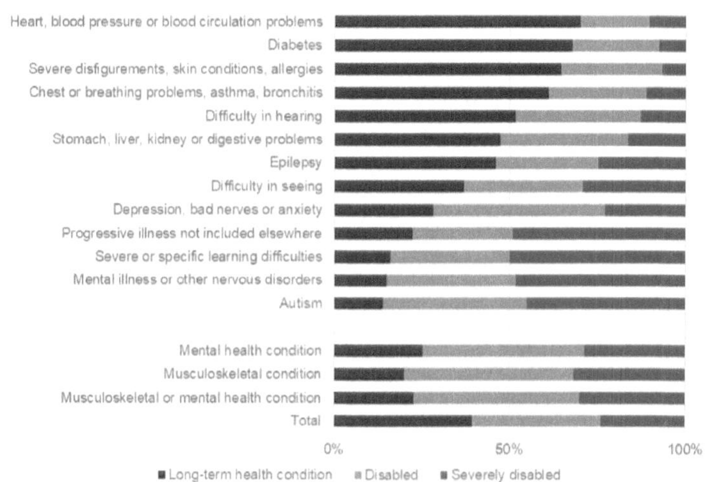

The unemployment rate for persons with a disability, at 10.1 percent in 2021, decreased

by 2.5 percentage points from the previous year but remained higher than in 2019 (7.3

percent). The jobless rate for those with a disability was about twice as high as for those without a disability.

(Unemployed persons are those who did not have a job, were

available for work, and were actively looking for a career in the four weeks preceding the survey.)

The unemployment rate for persons without a disability decreased by 2.8 percentage points to 5.1 percent in 2021.

Time spent on the internet/TV

Time spent watching TV or surfing the internet contributes significantly to mental and physical health. Staying glued to the screen can cause eye problems. Also, using the internet or watching TV prevents us from staying physically active. While there is a reasonable reduction in the percentage of people using TV nowadays, the truth is these people are not leaving the TV for some outdoor fun activities; they're going online instead.

The Internet is a new world with many booming and engaging activities, even when some of these activities are not beneficial to us. It's almost impossible to stay a day off the net and take good care of your mental and physical health. The growing interest in this has caused several health complications for a lot of people, both mentally and physically.

Time spent on the internet is of great importance to your body weight since you may spend a whole day checking Instagram pictures, engaging your followers on Twitter, or replying to friends on Facebook.

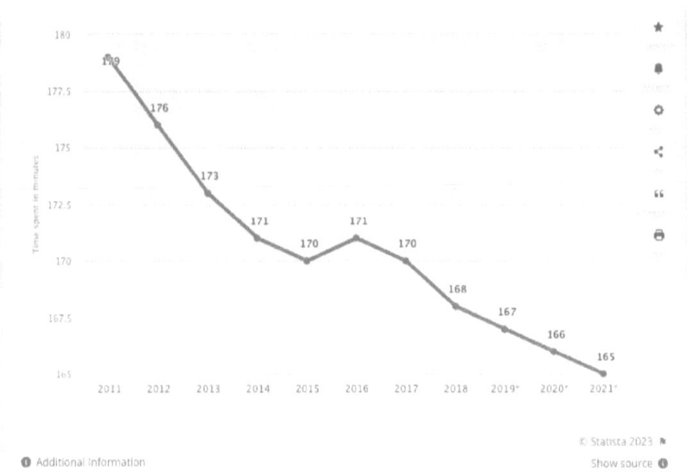

As presented by Statista, the chart shows a significant reduction in the time the global population spent watching TV every day. The decrease in the number of people using the TV is only a positive development when compared alone. However, the advent of the internet changed this position since more and more people now use the internet instead of TV.

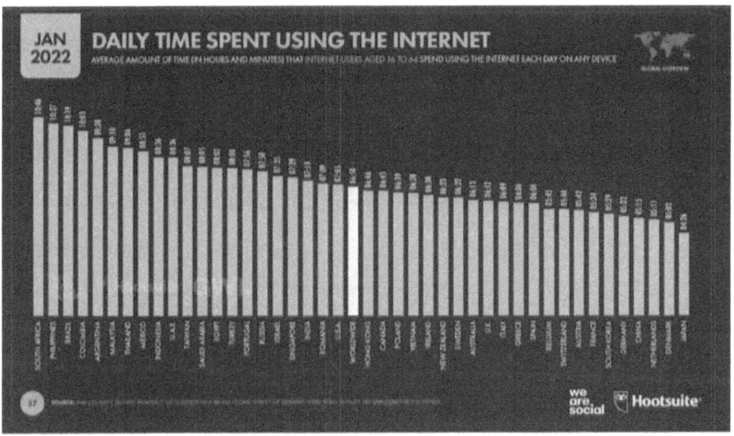

The internet is everywhere, from the deep of Africa to America, Asia, and Europe. Above 50% of the global population uses social media and the internet daily. The above chart shows South Africa as the leading country with the highest amount of time spent on the internet daily by its citizens.

Another form of the internet is video games. The industry has boomed more, thanks to the coronavirus pandemic in 2020. With stay-at-home advisories and lockdown directives in many countries, video games and eSports have become mainstream entertainment options among all age groups. The COVID-19 pandemic has shown that video games are not only played for entertainment or escapism, and many players use games as a source of income through video games that come with the play-to-earn mode. Also, playing video games has become an ideal way to connect with friends remotely and to socialize online.

A seemingly never-ending selection from casual games to indie releases to AAA blockbuster releases translates to a billion-dollar global market. Players can pick from gaming systems, with PCs and consoles like the Sony PlayStation, the Nintendo Switch, or Microsoft's Xbox being popular. However, despite the prominence of console gaming, mobile games account for the most significant share of the gaming market.

Based on current data, the average gamer is spending 8.6 hours per week playing video games, which equates to roughly 1.2 hours per day.

If the average of 8.6 hours per week stays consistent throughout an entire year, the total time spent playing video games in one year would add up to **two and a half weeks**.

Assuming that the same numbers stayed consistent throughout someones entire adult life, the total gaming playtime would equate to **2.8 years, which is ~4% of a person's lifetime**.

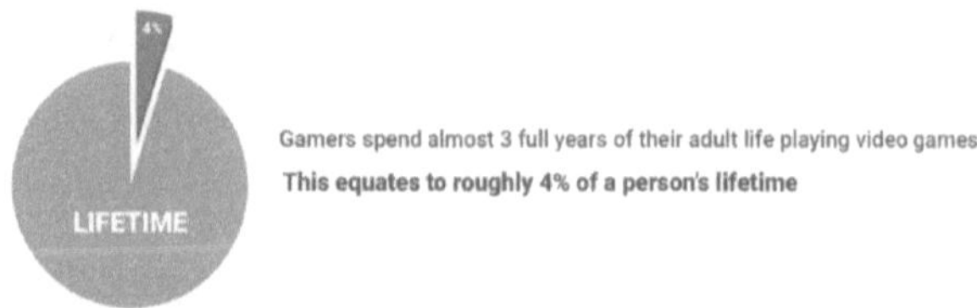

Gamers spend almost 3 full years of their adult life playing video games
This equates to roughly 4% of a person's lifetime

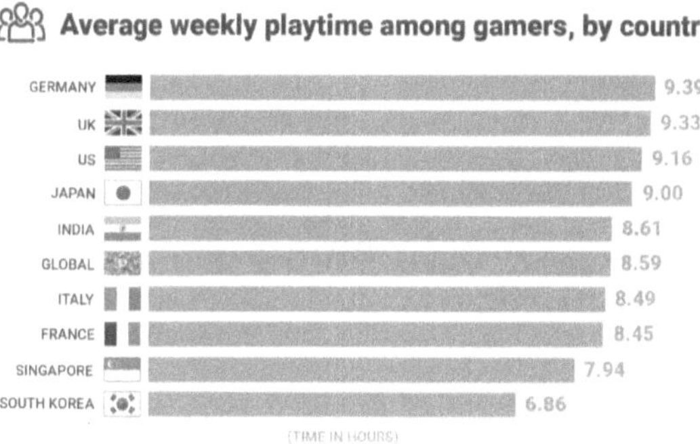

While the above charts show the number of hours spent playing video games by average players, the truth is video games can be very addictive and may require a lot of commitment to make a conscious effort to stop playing.

Video games are fun activities that can keep you in one position (sitting) without the requirement for physical activities, making it hard to burn more calories and may lead to gaining more weight in a brief period.

The introduction of the play-to-earn gaming model has made video games a form of addiction that comes with financial remuneration. Given that unemployment is a hard reality in many countries, it becomes even more impossible for players of this model to stop playing since that means they stop earning too.

However, we need to teach fitness into a part of our lives. Staying physically active transcends the mere act of being awake and requires constant servicing like your car. We must take good care of our bodies and stick to a certain morning exercise routine.

Addiction to Smoking or Alcohol consumption

Incessant smoking causes severe mental and physical illness; however, this is not the end. The tobacco epidemic is one of the biggest public health threats the world has ever faced, killing more than 8 million people a year, including around 1.2 million deaths from exposure to second-hand smoke.

Smoking or getting exposed to tobacco is unsafe. Hence, even without smoking, a person may suffer some health consequences simply for exposure to it. Cigarette smoking is the most common form of tobacco use worldwide. Other tobacco products include waterpipe tobacco, smokeless tobacco, cigars, cigarillos, roll-your-own tobacco, pipe tobacco, bidis, and kreteks.

Over 80% of the 1.3 billion tobacco users worldwide live in low- and middle-income countries, where the burden of tobacco-related illness and death is heaviest. Tobacco use contributes to poverty by diverting household spending from basic needs such as food and shelter to tobacco.

The economic costs of tobacco use are substantial. They include high healthcare costs for treating the diseases caused by tobacco use as well as the lost human capital that results from tobacco-attributable morbidity and mortality.

Smoking rates by country 2022

Country	Total Smoking rate
Nauru	52,1%
Chile	44,7%
Greece	39,1%
France	34,6%
South Africa	31,4%
Russia	28,3%
Germany	28,0%
Spain	27,9%
India	27,0%
United States	25,1%
China	24,7%
United Kingdom	19,2%
Canada	17,5%
Australia	16,2%

Source: World Health Organization

The chart shows the prevalence of smoking in our current world. Smoking can be a form of addiction or random habit, and it is another leading cause of mental health illness today. With more adults taking different forms of tobacco, smoking is becoming an acceptable means of life to escape safe realities or feel among their peers.

The major concern regarding tobacco smoking is that it may lead to mental and physical illness. Smoking generally exposes the victim to several harms, including addiction, reduced life span, and even more problems for the victim and the community.

Alcohol

According to the World Health Organization, there is a direct correlation between the level of alcohol consumption and the life expectancy of a person. Japan and France are considered the first and third countries with high life expectancy, respectively. Furthermore is supposed to consume less pure alcohol.

Country consumption statistics:
Japan has the gighest average life expectancy and consumes around one liter less of pure alcohol compared to the average.
Russia has the second lowest life expectancy out of the top countries, drinks the second most liters of pure alcohol, and is a high risk country on the WHO patterns of drinking index.

The countries with the most years of life lost due to Alcohol by annual number of liters consumed per person.

Country	Years of life lost due to drinking
Belarus	14,4
Lithuania	12,1
Czech Republic	11,8
France	11,8
Russia	11,5
Ireland	11,4
Portugal	11
Finland	10

The top 10 Countries by liters alcohol consumed

Country	Liters consumed
Belarus	14,4
Lithuania	12,9
Grenada	11,9
Czech Republic	11,8
France	11,8
Russia	11,5
Ireland	11,4
Luxembourg	11,4
Slovakia	11,4
Germany	11,3
United States	8,7

On the other hand, Belarus, Lithuania, France, and Russia are considered to be those with the highest loss of life expectancy due to heavy consumption of alcohol. A person in Belarus is estimated to consume about 14 liters of alcohol annually.

The correlation between life expectancy and alcohol consumption doesn't seem to be a positive one. Drinking wine in moderation may benefit some people's heart health, but stopping at just one glass isn't always as easy as it seems. Staying sober is difficult, and living in a country where alcohol is a major part of the culture can make sobriety even more challenging. Identifying the problem is the first step, but finding the suitable treatment facility and approach to fit your needs can be just as tough.
Another main concern here is that heavy consumption of alcohol, particularly beer, can add a very high level of sugar to the body system resulting in more calories, overweight, obesity, and even a big belly in some heavy drinkers. While many people focus on the ability to drink moderately, it is indeed hard to stop at one bottle glass is not usually considered until we start to see the

consequential result, which is a big belly and adding more weight.

"Healthy citizens are the greatest asset any
country can have."
–**Winston Churchill**

Why we die

For a long time, we've been made to believe that death comes naturally to everybody, so at one point in my life, I had faith in this belief that I do not think there could be any causative agents or factors at all.

Yes, death can come naturally to some people; however, contrary to the general view that all deaths are natural, some are caused by other factors and could be prevented or delayed with proper care and attention.

The world's biggest killer is ischemic heart disease, responsible for 16% of worldwide deaths. Since 2000, the largest increase in deaths has been caused by this disease, rising by more than 2 million to 8.9 million deaths in 2019. Stroke and chronic obstructive pulmonary disease are the 2nd and 3rd leading causes of death, responsible for approximately 11% and 6% of total deaths, respectively.

Lower respiratory infections remained the world's most deadly communicable disease, ranked the 4th leading cause of death. However, the number of fatalities has decreased substantially: in 2019, it claimed 2.6 million lives, 460 000 fewer than in 2000.

Neonatal conditions are ranked 5th. However, deaths from neonatal conditions are one of the categories for which the global decrease in deaths in absolute numbers over the past two decades has been the greatest: these conditions killed 2 million newborns and young children in 2019. Fortunately, there were 1.2 million fewer cases than in 2000.

Deaths from non-communicable diseases are on the rise. Trachea, bronchus, and lung cancer deaths have risen from 1.2 million to 1.8 million and are now ranked 6th among leading causes of death.

In 2019, Alzheimer's disease and other forms of dementia ranked as the 7th leading cause of death. Women are disproportionately affected. Globally, 65% of deaths from Alzheimer's and other forms of dementia are women.

One of the most significant declines in the number of deaths is from diarrhea diseases, with global deaths falling from 2.6 million in 2000 to 1.5 million in 2019.

Diabetes has entered the top 10 causes of death, following a significant percentage increase of 70% since 2000. Diabetes is also responsible for the largest rise in male deaths among the top 10, with an 80% increase since 2000.

Leading causes of death globally

At a global level, 7 of the 10 leading causes of deaths in 2019 were noncommunicable diseases. These seven causes accounted for 44% of all deaths or 80% of the top 10. However, all noncommunicable diseases together accounted for 74% of deaths globally in 2019.

Leading causes of death globally

2000   2019

1. Ischaemic heart disease
2. Stroke
3. Chronic obstructive pulmonary disease
4. Lower respiratory infections
5. Neonatal conditions
6. Trachea, bronchus, lung cancers
7. Alzheimer's disease and other dementias
8. Diarrhoeal diseases
9. Diabetes mellitus
10. Kidney diseases

0   2   4   6   8   10

Number of deaths (in millions)

Noncommunicable   Communicable   Injuries

Source: WHO Global Health Estimates.

Annual number of deaths from select risk factors worldwide
(in millions)

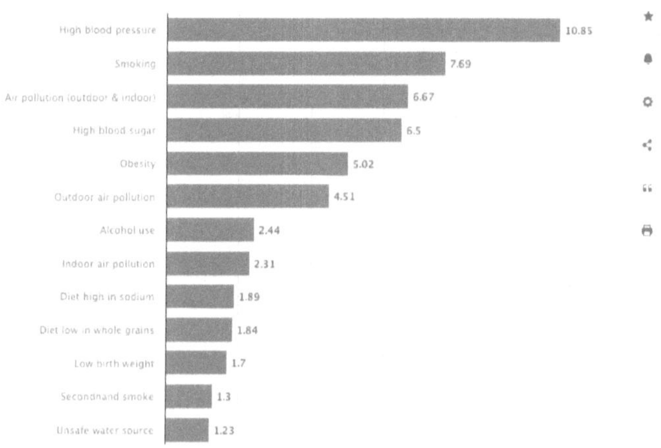

With a single look at the above chart, it's become apparent that several factors cause death or expose us to death. Obesity is said to occasion 5.02 percent of death every year, and factors like high blood pressure, smoking, pollution, and alcohol consumption caused 10.85, 7.69, 6.67, and 2.44 percent of death, respectively. There is also a need to add in a good diet as a lack of certain nutrients or overconsumption of certain nutrients can be caused death as well. For instance, overconsumption of meals with sodium is said to cause 1.89 percent of death, while diets that are low in grains reportedly cause 1.84 percent of death.

My parents

Two weeks before Christmas in 2011, I was talking with my mother. This year we were going to be together on Christmas eve, which was a massive event for her since it was the first time in many years. She was worried about my father; his health was not good. Years of smoking, inactivity and high intake of alcohol had given him several challenges. And she was concerned that he would be hospitalized and the Christmas for both of them was destroyed. They had been married for 40 years and had always been together.

The following day, I woke up with several missing calls from my parent house. Assuming something had happened to my father, I called back.

My father took the phone, telling me my mother had passed away that night. Years with overweight, high alcohol intake, and smoking had made her heart stop at age 67.

Sleep

Sleep deprivation is a condition that occurs if you don't get enough sleep. Sleep deficiency is a broader concept that captures any of the conditions below:

- You don't get enough sleep (sleep deprivation)
- You sleep at the wrong time of day
- You don't sleep well or get all the different types of sleep your body needs
- You have a sleep disorder that prevents you from getting enough sleep or causes poor-quality sleep

Sleeping is a basic human need, like eating, drinking, and breathing. Like these other needs, sleeping is vital for good health and well-being throughout your lifetime.

According to the Centers for Disease Control and Prevention, about 1 in 3 adults in the United States reported not getting enough rest or sleep every day. Nearly 40% of adults report falling asleep during the day without meaning to at least once a month. Also, an estimated 50 to 70 million Americans have chronic or ongoing sleep disorders.

Sleep deficiency can interfere with work, school, driving, and social functioning. You might have trouble learning, focusing, and reacting. Also, you might find it hard to judge other people's emotions and reactions.

Sleep deficiency also can make you feel frustrated, cranky, or worried in social situations.

Sleep deficiency is also linked to a higher chance of injury in adults, teens, and children. For example, sleepiness while driving (not related to alcohol) is responsible for serious car crash injuries and death. In older adults, sleep deficiency may be linked to a higher chance of falls and broken bones.

Sleep deficiency has also played a role in human mistakes linked to tragic accidents, such as nuclear reactor meltdowns, the grounding of large ships, and plane crashes.

A common myth is that people can learn to get by on little sleep without adverse effects. However, research shows that getting enough quality sleep at the right times is vital for mental health, physical health, quality of life, and safety.

An ongoing lack of sleep has been closely associated with hypertension, heart attacks and strokes, obesity, diabetes, depression and anxiety, decreased brain function, memory loss, weakened immune system, lower fertility rates, and psychiatric disorders.

5 Effects of Long-Term Sleep Deprivation
Hypertension

Sleeping less than 5 to 6 hours per night has been linked to elevated hypertension. Because sleep helps our bodies regulate hormones that cause stress, a lack of rest can amplify the effects of stress on the body. Long-term sleep deprivation is associated with increased blood pressure, heart rate, and inflammation. All of this puts unnecessary strain on your heart.

Heart Attack & Stroke

Sleep deficiency causes a greater instance of fatal cardiovascular problems, such as heart attacks and stroke. Doctors and researchers believe this is because the lack of sleep may disrupt the parts of the brain that control the circulatory system or cause inflammation that makes developing a blood clot more likely.

Weight Gain & Obesity

The effects of continual sleep problems include rapid weight gain. A lack of sleep is related to higher amounts of cortisol, a stress hormone; the resulting anxiety, stress, and frustration often contribute to emotional eating and poor nutritional habits. Another hormone, called ghrelin, is produced in the stomach and has been associated with long-term sleep deprivation; an excess of ghrelin can make people feel hungrier.

Over time, sleep deprivation negatively impacts the body's metabolism and eating habits. Tiredness often leads to unhealthy cravings, overindulgence, and decreased stamina and physical activity. Research has shown that people who feel unrested are more likely to choose foods rich in carbohydrates and sugar.

Mathematics tells us that a decrease in exercise, combined with an increase in the amount eaten plus an increase in the caloric value of the food ingested, equals weight gain. Obesity is a known risk factor for insomniacs.

Diabetes

Getting as much as 5 hours of sleep at night is still not enough. Research has shown that sleep deprivation may disrupt the body's method for processing glucose, which cells use for fuel, and the amount of insulin that the body produces. This is why it's a significant risk factor for developing type 2 diabetes.

Depression & Anxiety

Most people feel irritable if they haven't had a good night's sleep, but long-term sleep deprivation has been linked to clinical depression and a more general loss of motivation. Those dealing with depression are often found to an irregular sleeping patterns, which affects their mood considerably. The melatonin hormone controls mood regulation and the sleep cycle, and a lower level of melatonin is found in those dealing with depression or insomnia.

Furthermore, anxiety, fear, and panic attacks are three mental health illnesses connected to sleeping deficiency. However, while sleeping deficiency can result in several mental illnesses, patients dealing with mental health issues may also experience sleeplessness due to the mental issue. Thus, it is not necessarily the other way around.

"It is health that is the real wealth,
and not pieces of gold and silver."

Mahatma Gandhi

What to do?

Eat food. Your body needs it. The idea that you need to cut down on food to maintain your body is not entirely right. While intermittent fasting can help deal with insulin resistance and reduce your craving, your body requires a certain amount of energy to carry out daily functions. These calories can be consumed from food and fruit for proper results and nutrients

Even for someone who does not go to work or do a lot of hard work, a lot of energy is consumed by the eye for seeing alone. Hence, if you are thinking about losing weight, you should not be considering marathon fasting since that can affect your general well-being.

While eating is good for your body, overeating or binge eating is the reason we add more calories. Now the problem is not about adding calories; it is all about the tasks we put in place to burn those calories.

When you eat, your body turns calories into energy and allows you to function correctly. The level of energy required will largely base on the level of work you carry out per day. Generally, an adult should eat food containing 2000 calories. However, more calories may be required if you work more than an average adult.

How to distribute 2000 calories without necessary missing your breakfast or excellent snacks

- Breakfast: 300 kcal (15%)
- Snack: 200 kcal (10%)
- Lunch: 400 kcal (20%)
- Snack: 200 kcal (10-15%)
- Dinner: 600 kcal (25-30%)
- Evening: 300 kcal (15%)

Food to consider when making a plan on what to eat and the level of calories to be consumed may vary from different person to another; however, confirming the level of calories contained in the food before eating it can help tailor your daily meals to meet your energy requirement.

How many calories are there in some of the common foods we eat:

- 2 dl ready-cooked pasta (100 g): 150 kcal

- 2 dl ready-cooked rice (160 g): 160 kcal

- 1 salmon fillet (125 g): 170 kcal

- 2 fish cakes (100 g): 110 kcal

- 1 chicken fillet (90 g): 110 kcal

- 2 carrots (130 g): 50 kcal

- 1 small bowl of mixed salad (100 g): 20 kcal

Now compare the food to this

- Big Mac (Mc Donald's): 495 kcal

- Quarter Pounder (McDonald's): 505 kcal

- Cheese sausage w/bacon at the gas station: 350 kcal

- Coca Cola (0.5 litre): 210 kcal

- Potato crisps 280 gr. (Maarud): 1286 kcal

- Frozen Pizza (1/2): 500-650 kcal

How to burn calories?

Burning calories is not a complicated or easy thing; it is all about focusing on your goal and staying consistent with it.

For a male or Female weighing 65-70 kilos, the list of exercises below can be an excellent way to lose weight and live without the risk of obesity.

- Light exercise: 30 minutes of brisk walking - 200 kcal
- Moderate exercise: 30 minutes jogging/swimming - 350 kcal
- Complex training: 30 minutes running/spinning/cross fit - 500 kcal

Is Eating Healthy Expensive?

Many people believe that eating healthy is expensive when in the real sense, it is quite affordable. Of course, going grocery shopping may appear a little more expensive when you're buying everything; however, this naturally safe you from buying a lot of random food that cost far more.

- 2 dl ready-cooked pasta (100 g): 0,4 USD
- 2 dl ready-cooked rice (160 g): 0,2 USD
- 1 salmon fillet (125 g): 2 USD

- 2 fish cakes (100 g):1,2 USD

- 1 chicken fillet (90 g):1 USD

- 2 carrots (130 g): 0,3 USD

- 1 small bowl of mixed salad (100 g): 2 USD

Compare the above prices to the ones below

- Big Mac (Mc Donald's): 5,99 USD

- Quarter Pounder (McDonald's): 4,99 USD

- Cheese sausage w/bacon (gas station): 4 USD

- Coca Cola (0.5 litre): 1,5 USD

- Potato crisps 280 gr.: 2 USD

- Frozen Pizza (1/2): 4 USD

In our house, we start the day with oatmeal, with a little sugar and cinnamon on top. A packet of oatmeal costs 2 USD and lasts for a week for 5 people. It is a healthy and good alternative, which is also very cheap.

A healthy diet is varied and consists of more fruit and berries, vegetables and coarse grain products, and limited amounts of processed meat, red meat, salt, and sugar.

A good place to start is to focus on what you can eat more of, with that, there will automatically be less room for what you can eat.

How can I Follow the Dietary Advice?

It is not always easy to turn theory into practice. Focus on eating regularly and have a varied diet. A healthy diet is something you should be able to live with for the rest of your life, not just for a short period. Take the dietary advice as a starting point and think about what you think is easiest to eat in the morning. And what can you put in the lunchbox that makes you look forward to lunchtime?

Make a plan instead of a goal.

Do not set a goal that you are going to eat more fish. But plan for it instead.
If you want to start eating more fish, then make a plan. If you plan to eat fish on Mondays, Wednesdays, and Fridays, then you know what to do. You buy in and have that for dinner those days. Following a plan is easy.

Exercise
The WHO recommends being moderately physically active for at least 150 minutes per week, at least 30 minutes per day, five days a week. Moderate activity means activities that cause faster breathing than usual, for example, fast walking.

The recommendation can also be met with at least 75 minutes of high-intensity activity per week or a combination of moderate and high intensity.

- 2/3 of adults do NOT meet the recommendations for physical activity.

Why should you train again?

Because your body is by far your most important and most valuable asset!

How to get started with training?

- Find activities you think are fun.
- Set aside 30 minutes per day; a little is better than nothing.
- Plan and retrieve information.
- A training partner or training environment makes it more accessible.
- Find out what motivates you.
- Set realistic and measurable goals.
- Give yourself a slow start. This is supposed to be the race of a lifetime.

Does training need to be time-consuming?

- Walk/cycle to/from work.
- Go to the store when you shop.
- Go for a walk with friends.
- Exercise while watching TV
- Swim before working hours

Is 2.5 hours per week a lot for our most important asset? Make exercise a habit.

Does training need to be expensive?

- Your local parks are open and accessible all year round.
- Membership in a running club is never expensive
- A meet-up with your friends for a walk 2 times a week is free
- Park runs are being arranged all over the world, with free entrance.

8 good reasons to exercise

- You look better naked ;-)
- Exercise reduces stress
- Exercise gives you more energy
- Exercise improves self-confidence
- Exercise strengthens the immune system
- Exercise makes you more persistent
- Exercise prevents and reduces anxiety and depression
- Exercise improves sleep quality

- It is not necessary to train hard to get better health. Small adjustments in your activity level can have a significant impact on both your physical and mental health. The most important thing is to sit less still.

-

- Let light activities become part of the everyday routine. Choose activities that you like and that you feel you can do. If you feel yourself getting a little out of breath, the effect is better than a leisurely walk.

Early to bed, and early to rise,
makes a man healthy,
wealthy and wise.

Benjamin Franklin

Sleep

- Sleep difficulties are one of the most common health problems in the population.
- Approximately one in three adults struggle weekly with sleep.
- How much we sleep and how much sleep we actually need varies.
- There are large individual differences in sleep needs.
- For adults, it is normal to sleep between six and eight hours per night.

Sleep works best when we go to bed and get up at roughly the same time every day. While simple naps can be good during a break, deep sleep is required for proper mental positioning and to improve cognitive ability and overall efficiency. However, good and deep sleep does not just come. How well you sleep depends primarily on how long it has been since you last slept.

Thus, you should limit sleeping during the day to get good and continuous sleep at night. You can also increase the level of your physical activity to enhance a deep and blissful sleep at night.

Mental Health

Life goes up and down for most people. Everyday life consists of both good and bad experiences that make you feel good or less good.

Suppose you feel down, unsuccessful, scared, angry, or have other negative emotions that dominate your everyday life over time. In that case, it is important to remember that it is possible to reverse this.

What affects our mental health?

While the main reason you are sad may not be largely related to some of the things I want to mention here, the fact remains that you feel the effect of the main causes of your depression. However, some other factors may set in to shift your mind into that mode where you can accommodate sadness.

- **Proximity to other people:**
  The closer you are to people, the less chance you have to entertain sad feelings and negativities. Yes, sad times will come; however, you can easily overcome them if you pay more attention to yourself and keep more people around.

I notice that I do a lot of unhelpful thinking when I'm alone, which sometimes makes me sad; however, overcoming this is always easy whenever I hang out with friends or stay close to

my wife. It is easy to forget sad news or bad feelings when you are around people who can make you smile, talk or play.

- **A place to live:**
A certain level of your burden will disappear when you have a stable place to live. Living with friends and family can be more fun. However, some people enjoy the comfort of being alone, and having some private time can also be more beneficial to their mental health.
- **Enough food:**
Having enough food to eat signifies financial freedom. Not eating enough through financial constraints or intentional fasting can affect your mental health. Lack of food means low energy, which can lead to several symptoms of mental health issues, including apathy, tiredness, dizziness, and more.

- **Financial stability:**
  It's no news that financial ability goes a long way in determining how happy a person is and how lively they are among people. Financial freedom or stability is a big deal, and the ability to afford certain necessities can lead to mental health illnesses like depression, anxiety, and more.
- **Having something meaningful to do:**
  Living purposefully allows us to embrace fulfillment and happiness. With a mindset determined to get things done, we can live every day with the hope of achieving our goals or dreams, which can be a great way to boost mental health.

If you constantly feel tired or living or sad, there is a chance that you're not focusing your time on finding something meaningful. Create a purpose for your life and start living every day to actualize that purpose. In no time, you're likely to forget about the pain, grieve and embrace a more refreshed mental health.

Just as exercise helps if you're out of shape, talking to someone helps if you're struggling. Although many know it is important, it can be difficult to do it. The best way is to talk to a stranger because you will be less judged or controlled. Also, a stranger does not need to hear about the good things happening in your life. You can tell them about your pain, and they can listen without judgment.

- **Believe in yourself:**
  Until you start seeing your own light, no one can see it. Hence, it takes believing in yourself to see people who will also believe in you. Self-confidence is a good way to send away bad vibes. At a time when you're feeling down or unhappy, I know it can be hard to tell yourself it's okay and stay in control; however, it's important to let go of any inferior feelings and focus more on your innate ability to overcome all the pain and life a free life.

  Emotions have a purpose. Listen to what the body is trying to tell us. Accept that you have a problem. Talk about it to those who care to listen.

- **Do something nice daily**:
  "Fake it until you make it." Spending a nice time out, enjoying good and healthy meals, and participating in fun activities contribute to mental freedom. If you want to free yourself from the pain, you need to let go and laugh more.

If you find that problems persist over time and you are unable or unwilling to do what you usually do, you should seek help. (the doctor is the first stop)

Everyone has a mental health

Mental health is about how you perceive yourself and others, how you feel in everyday life, and how you cope with challenges. It is entirely normal to have psychological challenges from time to time, days, or periods when you find it more demanding to cope with everything around you. What does it take for you to feel positive emotions?

You can strengthen your mental health with these five steps:

- Create social ties
- Be active
- Be aware
- Continue to learn
- Give to others

And remember, even if you set high standards for yourself, you have no right to do so for others. Be generous with those around you.

*"Nurturing yourself is not selfish –
it's essential to your survival and your well-being."*
Renee Peterson Trudeau

My 5 life hacks that guarantee you a better and longer life.

Remember that the body is our most important asset

1. Avoid being overweight (BMI 20-25)

Now you have seen the consequences of overweight of mortality, physical and mental health. If you are overweight, it is time to take action.

Create a plan that is long-term and feasible for the rest of your life.

Start by reducing your intake of high-calorie foods and increasing your activity level. A little walk is better than no walk.

Reward yourself when you deserve it.

2. Eat healthy and regularly.

Make simple plans for when and what to eat and follow the plan. When, as it will happen, you have a deviation from the plan, get back to the plan as soon as possible.

Be patient and the results will come.

3. Exercise at least 150 minutes per week.

Set aside an hour 3 times per week.

Do something you think is fun, and preferably with others.

If you can't think of anything, go for a walk at a moderate pace.

Look for openings in everyday life to increase your activity level.

Our nature is a fantastic arena that is always open and free.

4. Create good, close communities.

Be generous with those around you, and also yourself.

Even if you have high expectations for yourself, you have no right to demand the same from others.

Look for the positive qualities in the people around you.

And take joint active initiatives

5. Find your balance between work - rest, and play.

Sleep and rest is essential for a good life.

A healthy balance could be: meeting your deadlines at work while still having time for friends and hobbies. Having enough time to sleep properly and eat well. not worrying about work when you're at home.

Conclusion

TAKE CARE OF YOURSELF AND YOUR CAR.

What I drive today.

With 3 kids in the back seat and an active life, I ended up with an SUV. My blue Land Rover Discovery Sport is perfect, both practical and with a nice design. With 4-wheel drive, we can get to the mountain and ski in the wintertime, and I can bring my road bike around in the summertime. A large engine makes it sporty, safe, and fun to drive.

Since I got my Golf in 1992, there has been the introduction of new cars and discoveries. However, I realize choosing an SUV car is a practical decision; when combined with good maintenance, you can enjoy a lovely ride with the people around you.

The case is similar for your body. Taking good care of who you are and exploring several tips to enhance your body is a good way to live longer without medical treatment or surgeries. Life will not always be a bed of roses; however, we can overcome its turns and live happily with our decisions.

Starting now is the best option to get in shape and live a happy life with your body. Irrespective of where your body goal is right now, understanding that you can achieve more result is a way of showing you that living in a good body does not necessarily starts at 17. Hence, your age has no impact on this. Take the very first step by being free from mental health burdens, explore and enjoy fitness tips with freedom, and taking a conscious step to improve yourself.

Thanks to all of you for supporting me in my daily life. I hope you read every part with an open mind, ready to pick up new behaviors, appreciate new tips, and enjoy your life in a healthier body. Whether you're at 50 or somewhere near that, you can still achieve great improvement, and I wait to hear that "**you did it**" without taking your age or mindset as hindrances.

Change is not easy; however, with the right inspiration, you can get it done. There may be times when you're indifferent or suddenly tired of going. Daily exercise may cause you some frustration, and lack of instant results may reduce your everyday motivation, but I need you to keep going without looking back. You've left the stage when your mind is carefree about the decisions you made and how they affect your body;

hence, you cannot afford to be indifferent towards your body or car now.

"A fit body, a calm mind, a house full of love. These things cannot be bought – they must be earned."

Naval Ravikant

Acknowledgements

To my family.

Thank you, my awesome wife, Siv Therese.
You make me a better person, and my life a more colorful place. Trude, my sister, for being the person I always can turn to. My biggest gift in life, my kids. Anine, Aurora, Mathias, Gabriel and Emma. You are the sun in my heaven. And my little angels, Agnes and June.

Sigurd Urdal, the man who gave me inspiration and helped me develop the presentation that ended up with this book.

My colleagues at Global Health Technology that every day drives to give more people increased quality of life.

Finally, I want to thank you for reading this book. A book without a reader has no value. I really hope you are inspired to do some changes that will give you a happier and better life. And if you liked the book, please tip someone you care about or lend them you copy.

"For he who has health has hope,
and he who has hope,
has everything"

Owen Arthur

Author's Bio

Alf Erik Malm is a keynote speaker, a father, a husband, and CEO of Global Health Technology. He has a background in medicine and marketing and has made it his mission to share his lifelong experiences and comprehensive research on the quality of life.

He is a lover of sports and an advocate for a healthy lifestyle, helping people from different walks of life to create suitable and healthy life hacks. From meal planning to proper sleep and mental positioning, He believes changing our lives for the better requires the first step to embrace ourselves, learn about the things we are taking for granted and improve on them without procrastination.

Helping others through forums, communities, and social events, Alf Erik has developed the ability to explain complex areas easily and motivate others has made him a popular speaker and consultant.

"A car – and the art of maintaining a body" is his debut book. He shared his document collection of life hacks that guarantee a better and longer life. The book is a result of 30 years of working in the field of giving people a better and longer life.

The author can be contacted on alf-erik@inore.no